D0908802

Chicago Public Library

REFERENCE

Form 178 rev. 1-94

CHICAGO PUBLIC LIBRARY

THE MISSOURI STATE FAIR

THE MISSOURI STATE FAIR

IMAGES OF A MIDWESTERN TRADITION

RICHARD GASKELL

UNIVERSITY OF MISSOURI PRESS
COLUMBIA AND LONDON

University of Missouri Press, Columbia, Missouri 65201

Printed and bound in Canada

Library of Congress Cataloging-in-Publication Data

Gaskell, Richard.

   The Missouri State Fair : images of a midwestern tradition / Richard Gaskell.

        p. cm.

   ISBN 0-8262-1273-5 (alk. paper)

    1. Missouri State Fair. I. Title.   00-020419

S555.M668 G37 2000

630'.74'778–dc21

Printer and binder: Friesens
Typefaces: Textile, Eras, Usherwood

FOR BENJAMIN AND CHRISTOPHER

Acknowledgments

Without the help and support of Herb and Louise Echelmeier of Higginsville, Missouri, this book would not have been possible. Over the years they have provided me with a home, food, transportation, pickups and deliveries at the airport, and at least a thousand kindnesses. I will always be grateful.

A number of special people have given their financial support to the project. Thanks to Ken Blumberg and Sarah Weinstein, Pat Casale and Gary Gut, Christine Collins, Constance Donovan, Gerry Dwyer and Cynthia Strout-Dwyer, Maura Fitzgerald, Mark Fowler, Mark and Martha Gregg, Jean and Russ Johnson, John and Mimi Jones, Margo and Andy Lane, Walter and Maureen Mercer, Lauren and David Murphy, Michelle and Dan Page, Linda Percy, Eric and Jane Philippi, Mercedes Ridao, Nedra and Gene Sahr, Barbara and Alan Shoolman, Dick and Cindy Vietor, Michael Ward, and Barbara and John Wicker.

Special thanks to my wife, Victoria, who became a single parent for the hottest two weeks of each summer and who has been a support and an encouragement through it all.

THE MISSOURI STATE FAIR

INTRODUCTION

Each year as the summer days drift lazily into August, I am reminded by the buzzing of cicadas that it will soon be fair time in Missouri, and I feel a delicious sense of anticipation, like a child eagerly awaiting an important holiday. For me, the persistent song of the cicadas has become a kind of ritual invitation to return once again to the Missouri State Fair. I am especially delighted to receive this invitation from such seasonal creatures because the Missouri State Fair is an institution devoted to the rituals of season and celebration of the harvest.

For as long as humans have tilled the soil, they have celebrated the harvest. European immigrants to the New World brought their traditional harvest rituals and festivals with them. These customs found expression in the community and county fairs that developed as America was settled. As roads and transportation developed, fairs were able to attract people from increasingly larger areas and thus grew larger themselves. As regions became territories and territories became states, groups of influential and wealthy people formed agricultural societies, eventually followed by state-supported agricultural societies that promoted state fairs as an ideal vehicle to showcase the bounty of the agriculture and industry of each state.

While state fairs were developing during the last half of the nineteenth century, the nation was undergoing unprecedented social and technological change. State fairs, because they were one of the few occasions when rural people gathered in large numbers, became a popular way to showcase new products, processes, and ideas. State fairs became more than just a place where rural people came to celebrate the familiar rituals of their lives—they became places to discover the new and marvelous.

Of course there has always been the entertainment. Horse racing in its various forms was an enormously popular attraction in the early days. And from the beginning, people have come to sell every conceivable gadget or novelty; at the fair, one could see hucksters, games of chance, freak shows, clowns, and circus performers. And there has always been an element of tension between these individuals and the interests promoting the "loftier" purposes of the fair. The *Sedalia Democrat*, in a description of the 1902 Missouri State Fair, was somewhat disdainful of people who came to the fair seeking only entertainment: "There were the usual sight-seers who came only to be amused, but there were also, in large numbers, intelligent Missourians who came to carefully study the exhibits and receive valuable information." The problem in the end, of course, was that without the entertainment people would not come out in sufficient numbers to assure the commercial success of the fair, and so the amusements were tolerated, if somewhat begrudgingly.

It is this confluence of timeless ritual, sober promotion of "scientific agriculture," and the sensational—even bizarre—that has given state fairs much of their unique character.

The first time I went to the Missouri State Fair was in 1968. I was serving as a VISTA (Volunteers in Service to America) volunteer in Boonville, Missouri, and a group of us drove to Sedalia; this was my first encounter with a large midwestern state fair. I was so captivated that I promised myself that I would return one day to photograph these people, their animals, and their fair. It wasn't until 1986 that I was able to fulfill that promise; in August of that year I boarded a plane in Boston and dropped out of the sky in Missouri, cameras in hand. I have been coming back ever since.

That year, my initial impression of the Missouri State Fair was that of a small city under an enormous sky. I had forgotten the sheer size of this spectacle: The Missouri State Fair covers 396 acres. I marveled at barns and buildings that were not merely constructed, but lovingly crafted of brick. Having adopted certain urban sensibilities during my years in Boston, I was amused to discover a magnificent building called a "Coloseum" devoted exclusively to the purpose of exhibiting animals. I saw ornamented buildings, structures built for a great purpose filled with all kinds of people. Old people, young people. Fat people and thin people. Ordinary people and outrageous people. People of the earth. I vividly remember the smells of the fair. Strong smells, sweet smells, pungent smells. Smells of corn dogs and smells of manure. On mornings after a rain these odors would combine with the freshness of the prairie breeze—and the resulting aroma can only be described as marvelous. The peace of the morning would be interrupted at regular intervals by a voice over the loudspeakers warning "Jimmy" that if he didn't find his way to the Highway Patrol office in five minutes, Mom and Dad might be going home with one less child; or a reminder that "Aunt May" would be meeting the kids at the Beef House for lunch at noon.

Some days the heat was oppressive. People sat in the shade or retreated into those few buildings that had air conditioning. Livestock people went about their obligatory tasks regardless of the heat, and the animals, when not in the arena, were provided with fresh bedding, penned in pleasant circumstance, and cooled by enormous fans. Animals here have always been the real celebrities, not people. The Missouri State Fair has forever redefined for me the meaning of the expression "creature comforts."

As state fairs go, the Missouri State Fair is something of a Johnny-come-lately. By the 1850s Ohio, Michigan, Minnesota, Illinois, Iowa, and Indiana all had state fairs of their own, and though an annual exhibition was attempted in Boonville in 1853, it failed after only three years. The St. Louis Agricultural and Mechanical Fair, inaugurated in 1856, was popular, but many small Missouri farmers were either reluctant or unwilling to exhibit their livestock in large cities. Missouri livestock competed with great success at the Chicago World's Fair in 1893, and this helped to reinforce the idea that Missouri really needed its own state fair in a centrally located rural Missouri community.

On January 29, 1899, a bill was introduced in the Missouri legislature calling for the establishment of a state fair. The bill was passed by a vote of 88 to 12 on April 5, 1899. Although the bill stipulated that the fair should be established in a community "easily accessible and well situated in the state," any town could compete to be the fair site. The competition was intense, but on October 10, 1899, Sedalia became the official site of the Missouri State Fair.

It had been intended initially to hold the first Missouri State Fair in 1900, but a lack of funds and time led organizers to postpone the first fair until 1901. Fifteen thousand dollars was appropriated for the fair by the Fortieth General Assembly, and an additional fifty thousand was appropriated by the Forty-first General Assembly on March 18, 1901.

September 9–14, 1901, were the dates determined for the first fair, leaving less than five months in which to make all preparations, including design and construction of drives and walks; extension of railroad spurs; grading of the race track; construction of a temporary grandstand, horse barn, and administration building; and erection of tents, water lines, and telephone connections. These tasks, however, were accom-

plished with two days to spare, and the fair opened on schedule. The *Sedalia Democrat* of September 9, 1901, gave an enthusiastic and detailed account of that first day.

> The Missouri State Fair, which opened today and will close Friday night, will furnish a gratifying surprise to all visitors. It will be larger and better than anyone has expected, and the magnitude of the fair, resulting from the strenuous labor of the members of the fair board during the past year, will be seen in the excellent and numerous exhibits in each department.

The first morning of the fair had involved a predictably large amount of hustle and bustle as participants arrived to register their entries, but by noon the exposition had settled down somewhat. The secretary of the fair was busiest of all, but he and his assistants "handled the work that crowded upon them in an admirable and expeditious manner." Meanwhile, no matter where he went, Superintendent Bast was constantly engaged by people wanting "privileges and concessions."

Other busy people included the workers at the telephone exchange, the Western Union telegraph office, and the post office, who "provided splendid service, furnishing up-to-date accommodations for the officials of the fair and the general public" in the administration building.

The *Sedalia Democrat* was careful to point out the presence of emergency services, including the fire department, whose "headquarters [was] admirably located near the cattle, horse and swine barns, . . . ready to promptly answer fire calls." In the days before electricity, when gaslights were the main form of illumination, even in straw-filled barns, this was an important consideration indeed.

The organizers had thought of everything; in addition to the fire department, the police were also there to help out, and an emergency hospital was set up near the administration building. Sharing that space was the Women's Christian Temperance Union (the W.C.T.U.), whose members were busy "sustaining their well earned reputation as most hospitable hostesses."

But those were just the support services; the "main event" was then, as it has always been, the animals. Thus, the *Sedalia Democrat* was proud to report that "the live stock show will be all and more than has been predicted for it. The entries cover a wide field and include the pick of the choicest herds of cattle, swine and sheep."

And a pleasant surprise for fairgoers was the broad variety and good condition of the animals in the poultry show:

> . . . the local fanciers did not expect a large exhibit of poultry on account of birds of the majority of breeds not being in show condition in the early part of September. A gratifying disappointment has been furnished, and the poultry show will be the biggest and best ever before seen in the state. In addition to the large number of exhibitors who made entries last week, a carload of birds came in this morning from Charleston, Ill., and another carload is expected this afternoon from Whitewater, Wis. Freak birds are numerous, including varied hued frizzled and silkies.

There was a good turnout in the horse barns that first year, too, including "light harness horses, jacks, jennets and mules," but there were "quite a number of stalls empty in the draft horse class"; thus, the decision was made to use that extra space for "overflow from the show horse department." Meanwhile, the cattle barns were "filled to overflowing" with beef cattle, and the dairy cattle, such as Jerseys, Holsteins, and others, were "provided with stalls under canvas."

The newspaper characterized the sheep and swine shows as "complete," with the "pick of the best herds in this country":

> Individual exhibitors of sheep and swine have flung to the breeze a multitude of blue ribbons, captured this year at the Nebraska, Iowa and Wisconsin State Fairs, these pretty tokens furnishing substantial evidence that the animals shown are of purest blood and the choicest products of careful and scientific breeding. Hundreds of sheep and swine are shown and the admirer of livestock will thoroughly enjoy the fine exhibition in the sheep building.

The art, horticultural, and textile exhibits were described in glowing terms as well; the newspaper congratulated the participants in and organizers of each display. Despite the drought that had afflicted gardeners that year, the flowers on display in 1901 still equaled "the best ever shown at a state fair." And the textile fabric exhibition had so many entries of fine needlework that organizers were forced to secure extra space if they were to show them all.

Other displays included the poultry stores, which the newspaper predicted would be "the center of attraction for the epicure . . . presenting a show which whets the appetite and inspires covetness"; and the agricultural department, which featured "numerous choice exhibits from Pettis and surrounding counties." The mineral and forestry exhibits presented products from all over the state, and the display of Missouri woods was "quite extensive and . . . well arranged for exhibition."

As with the fairs of today, entertainment was an important part of each day's events, but in 1901 it involved no electricity, no microphones: "The New Bloomfield band, in gorgeous uniforms of old gold and red, under the leadership of C. J. Howertine, appeared early at the grounds and from the bandstand furnished excellent music during the day." Additionally, "indigent street musicians, both male and female," attended the first fair "in large numbers," and the "'melodious' strains of hand organs, harps, etc., [were] heard on many corners. . . ."

And in 1901, as now, members of the younger generation found at the fair a special opportunity to take full advantage of the particular freedom that comes with outdoor activities. September 9, 1901, had been officially declared "Children's Day," and "the young folks turned out by the hundreds and thoroughly enjoyed themselves. They took full possession of the grand stand and the police had their hands full preventing their occupation of the race course."

The *Sedalia Democrat*'s account also described the weather of the first day of the Missouri State Fair, saying it "was all that could be desired for an opening day, being refreshingly cool, with the sun hid by hazy clouds. The showers of Sunday evening had completely settled the dust and placed the race track in almost a perfect condition for the trotting race." Describing the scene further, the newspaper continued: "The attendance was fully as large as had been expected for the first day and tomorrow visitors will pour through the turnstiles by the thousands. . . . The fair grounds are covered with big and little tents, and the space between the race track and the railway depots is well filled with dining halls and booths, privilege people of all kinds, implement displays and different kinds of shows, including snake eaters, 4,000-pound steers and the Australian colony."

Attendance at the first fair was 25,346 (it is not known whether the members of the "Australian colony" were counted in this total).

Nearly a hundred years later, in 1999, attendance was estimated at 343,207. Throughout the years the Missouri State Fair has grown and yet remained intimate, changed and yet remained the same. Through all the years it has lived up to the original catalog's prediction that

> The Missouri State Fair will be what Missourians make it. . . . It should be the greatest institution of the kind on earth. The fertility of our soil, the great variety of our products, extended deposits of valuable minerals, large areas of valuable forests, the superiority of our herds, and the progressive character of our citizenship warrant the management in anticipating a successful initial meeting and in predicting for the Missouri State Fair a future of usefulness to the state's industrial interests.

People have been coming to the fair for a hundred years. They come from all over the state and all over the Midwest. They come in automobiles and trucks, air conditioned and comfortable. But in the early days of the fair, people, livestock, exhibitors, and entertainment came by train, as the Missouri-Pacific and Missouri, Kansas & Texas railroads ran a spur right into the fairgrounds. And in the early days of the automobile, people traveled for many hours over dirt roads. Norwood Creason, an eighty-one-year-old member of the Missouri State Fair board of directors, has been coming to the fair for most of those years, but he vividly remembers making the journey in 1927:

> We started out in my dad's old Model T Touring [car] with Mom, Pop, and the four of us kids, and my grandfather and grandmother, my mother's folks, with a lot of camping equipment and stuff. We got about fifteen miles from home and hit a hole and blew a tire, and we stopped to put a spare on. A mile or so down the road, we hit another big hole. We drove dirt roads and we'd had some rain, you know, and they had the holes and they were rough—and my daddy was in kind of a hurry, and I guess he hit 'em a little too hard and blew another tire and broke the front spring—and he just turned off on an old dirt road toward Richmond and traded that Model T in on a brand new 1927 Chevy four-door for six hundred ninety-five dollars' difference. And then, of course, you had to break it in at twenty-five miles an hour, and we left Richmond sometime after noon, the middle of the afternoon I

> guess it was, and got in there at eleven o'clock. The longest ride I'd ever rode in my life. Uncomfortable as I could be.

Jim Riley, the sheep superintendent at the Missouri State Fair for twenty-five years, was a student in the agricultural school at the University of Missouri–Columbia in 1948:

> We loaded the sheep up in Hamilton, Missouri, about ten o'clock at night and arrived at the Missouri State Fair the first time in 1948 about two o'clock in the morning. My ag instructor, he was bringin' down a whole bunch of us, and he got us all together. We had the sheep and the hogs and the cattle all loaded, and then we had a caravan pulling down through here—and when we'd get in, the first thing we'd have to do is get everything strawed down and penned and fed, and by that time it would be about five-thirty or six in the morning. It was too late to go to bed, too early to get in trouble.

One or two of the old-timers can even remember people who brought themselves and their belongings to the fair in wagons pulled by teams of horses.

Traveling to the fair is certainly not the adventure it often was in the early days, but the fair itself is still quite an experience. Everywhere you look, people, products, animals, and machines are in competition to determine the best looking, best tasting, best made, the strongest, or the fastest. There are contests of strength in which men stack bales of hay or throw them over an ever-rising bar until only one is left to win the title of "super he-man farmer." There are truck and tractor pulls, lawn tractor pulls, antique and classic tractor pulls, draft horse pulls, and pony pulls. There are pig races and stock car races. There are competitions for best pickles and best jam. Technology has changed the look of certain events but not their basic flavor. Norwood Creason remembers the earliest tractor pulls:

> At that time, you just had a big old wooden sled and you piled up a bunch of concrete blocks on it . . . and then you'd line up a bunch of guys ten feet apart all the way up and down each side, and as you went by you'd step on the sled, and finally you'd get so many on there the tractor couldn't pull it. . . . These they've got now are very sophisticated. And they're much better than the ones where

people stepped on. . . . It's really pretty scientific. No hot rods or anything when they first started pulling. They just got 'em a tractor out of the field and started in pulling. Some of the guys got to really tuning 'em up. Now I had a very distant relative, Ben Creason, . . . and he had an Oliver 1650 [tractor], and Oliver has a big cast iron grille, and you pull in weight classes, you know, and he couldn't win in that weight class. So he took that grille off and made him a grille of real light wood, painted it, and it looked just like an Oliver grille. And it weighed about three or four pounds, where this other one was maybe two hundred and fifty pounds, and then that gave him an edge over most of 'em and he would win all of 'em with that wooden grille on there.

Some events, such as the draft horse pulls and pony pulls, are more popular now than they have ever been. People fill the Coloseum to see teams of horses compete until only one team is left to pull a weighted sled the required distance. A draft horse pull is mostly a quiet, orderly affair. Teams spend long minutes standing quietly in the soft earth, their drivers relaxed, waiting for their turn, but never losing track of other competitors. But when a team begins to pull, the atmosphere electrifies as chains snap taut and teams of two-thousand-pound horses strain with every ounce of strength they possess. Even the most casual observer can see right away that these horses just love to pull. The winning team is one that has worked together for some time with a driver who has a real understanding of and affection for his horses. Pony pulls are a miniature version of the draft horse pulls, with the ponies competing with all the heart of their larger cousins.

The best of everything is shown at the fair, but it is equally important for high quality to be consistent. Lloyd Alexander has shown hogs, sheep, and chickens over the past fifty years:

I remember I used to always show ten ears of corn at the county fair. Now if you was gonna win with them ten ears of corn, they had to be uniform and look exactly alike. Well, you'd go out to the field and I don't know how much corn I ruined findin' ten ears. . . . I'd end up maybe with twenty that I thought looked alike, and then I'd sort from them. And today, showin' trios [of chickens], I work quite a while to get . . . pullets or hens, whichever, lookin' just alike, because this goes back to my days in FFA

[Future Farmers of America] when the ag teacher said, "now you got to get three pullets that look alike," and of course you had to have ten ears of corn that looked alike. So, today yet, this is still instilled in my mind, that whenever you put more than one animal or thing together, they should look as near alike as you can possibly get 'em.

Even the time spent waiting to exhibit lent itself to competition. JoBill Reid, eighty-eight, tells of competition in the livestock barns sixty-five years ago:

There used to be some awful hot pitch games. A lot of us went to the fair to play pitch as much as to show sheep. We had an old racehorse man that took up sheep showing, and I wasn't allowed to gamble you know; didn't any of us have any money, anyway. We had bug races. You don't think about bug racin', do ya! Well, barn bugs are about so big . . . you know, black. There was seven of us in the barn had bugs, and we'd draw a line just like a terrapin race or anything, turn our bugs loose in the middle, and have a race. This happened every night during the fair. We had a lot of fun.

Although bug racing may be a thing of the past, there is one thing that hasn't changed from the very first fair: A day at the Missouri State Fair starts early. At daybreak the smell of ham, sausage, bacon, and eggs on the grill at Brockman's or the Mule Barn Grill carries across the fairgrounds. The sounds of electric shears and vacuums break the morning quiet as livestock are groomed with an attention to detail that would shame many an expensive salon. Animals are constantly coming and going from the barns as they are washed and groomed in preparation for show, people and animals mingling in a swirl of activity.

And it is not just animals that are groomed for show. Young exhibitors in particular are subject to critical examination by parents, who make sure that nothing is out of place. The dress code varies depending on the kind of livestock being shown. People showing beef cattle generally deck themselves out in western hats, jeans, cowboy boots, and of course an endless variety of eye-catching belt buckles. Dairy people often exhibit in white shirts and pants. Sheep people dress in everything from more formal western attire to jeans, T-shirts, and sneakers. Hog people almost invariably wear baseball-style caps, jeans, and T-shirts, or, in the case of the older generations, bib overalls and rubber boots or Wellingtons. The horse people array themselves in an endless variety of outfits from very simple western dress to the most elaborate formal English riding attire. However, perhaps the most eclectic of all are the mule people. The men, for example, can be found wearing everything from sharp western outfits, sporting waxed moustaches, to bib overalls with baseball caps and full beards.

In the Coloseum during the cattle judging, the class being judged will be at one end while others wait patiently for their classes to be called at the other end. Shafts of sunlight from upper-story windows highlight faces and features, and the occasional lowing of cattle punctuates the velvet quiet known only to buildings with earthen floors.

By ten o'clock fairgoers start to arrive in greater numbers, and the fair is ready to greet them. Street performers, clowns, and jugglers circulate among the crowd; around every corner there is a refreshment stand selling everything from funnel cakes and corn dogs to pizza, ribs, beer, and a host of other delightful substances to which the word *nutritional* only marginally applies. The Commercial and Varied Industries buildings draw crowds as vendors proclaim the virtues of knives that will never dull, pots and pans to which nothing will stick, and all manner of guaranteed-for-a-lifetime widgets, gadgets, and gizmos. You can buy an encyclopedia or a sewing machine and learn about the Catholics, Mormons, and Baptists—all under one roof. The children's barnyard is always a popular stop, and the Floriculture and Fine Arts buildings stand in a quiet corner, dignified in their white clapboarding.

By noon there is a line at the Pork Chop Place, the Missouri Beef House, and the Poultry Place. If there is a tractor or pickup pull at the State Fair Arena, the noise will carry across the entire grounds and plumes of black smoke can be seen from everywhere. If there are auto races in the grandstand, the noise can be deafening. Elsewhere, crowds gather to watch "Kachunga and the Alligator Show" or bungee divers leaping from a crane a hundred feet in the air. Everywhere there is the sound of music, mostly country, from the Bud Tent, Chuck and Dee's, Good Time Charlie's, or the Hacienda.

At midday, crowds are mingling everywhere, all kinds of people dressed in every conceivable outfit. The midway, of course, draws a crowd.

Everywhere you look, it's "three tries for a dollar" and "everyone's a winner." Although the burlesque shows are gone and the freak shows are toned down now in an attempt to be more "politically correct," the midway still manages to retain a sense of naughtiness that appeals to fairgoers of all ages.

On the wall in Brockman's Cafe, signed pictures of politicians, celebrities, and astronauts overlook the farmers, ranchers, carnies, and city folk who all sit down to eat together. The Republicans and the Democrats have tents filled with literature across from the grandstand, and people stop in to declaim with varying degrees of eloquence about the state of the nation or to complain about the other party. Politics is still a grassroots matter here.

With twilight, the fair becomes a place of magic, the fading light and thousands of colored incandescent lamps blending together to make the transition from day to night almost seamless. Laughter, exclamations, music from a concert in the grandstand, and a hundred other sounds ride the still evening air.

From the beginning I have been mesmerized by the fair as a feast for the senses. I also found a much deeper and enduring connection with the fair as I have become acquainted with the farm people who come to show their animals. Their relationship with their animals stirs something that lies deep within me and, I suspect, in all of us. Perhaps it is an ancient memory from a time when spirits were believed to live in the bodies of beasts and the purposes of other creatures were regarded as important. Whatever the reason, there is enduring magic in this relationship.

Farm people and their animals are more than simply the principal reason for the fair's existence: They are its life and breath. Showing livestock at the Missouri State Fair involves the entire family. FFA and 4-H programs are actively encouraged and supported. In many cases, involvement with animals begins almost as soon as a child learns to walk. It is not at all uncommon when showing a flock of sheep, for example, to have a small child pop up among them as if a part of the flock. I can think of very few other places where three or more generations of one family are all working together. It is always wonderful to see parents and children, and grandparents and grandchildren together, but to see parents and grandparents teaching and sharing with the children the traditions, values, and legacy of the family is quite extraordinary. The months of hard work in raising and preparing animals pay off for both young and old in the special excitement of showing at the fair.

Eloise Riley, wife of sheep superintendent Jim Riley, has been involved with young livestock exhibitors at the fair for many years. I asked her what the fair has meant to her and the people with whom she has worked:

> Well, it's my favorite time of the year. It's better than birthday and anniversary, Christmas, all the other days put together. It's a time when we see our friends. Our families are together. It's like a working vacation, but it's fun. We have friends that we sometimes don't see any other time of year, but it's camaraderie, togetherness — it might be meals together. We may cry at times. We laugh a lot, and we watch our children, and we watch our children come back with their families. It's a time that just really doesn't compare with any other particular activity at any other time.
>
> When the children go home, they go back to school, and they're always several measures stronger, more confident. They're more at ease in a lot of ways. They remember good times and they almost always want to come back. And they grow up some, too, while they're here. Some of the children will bring a wether that they have worked with all summer long that they've become very close to. They've groomed and led, stretched, competed with their best of friends and their toughest of competitors. . . .
>
> It's a growing experience. It's an enrichment. It's a learning experience. It's sportsmanship when it's hard to do, and it's something that I think becomes inbred in them later. Some of the things that you learn in younger life will stay with you for a long time, and that's part of what we strive to do. To teach fairness and remember that somebody else can also win and that if you did your best with your best possibility then that's what is expected of you. . . .
>
> It's a special time when you're young at heart. I think that's why I still love the fair. I don't think I'll ever feel any different about it. It's all right to have an affair with the fair.

Watching children show livestock is without a doubt one of my favorite pastimes at the fair. Pig drives are a great example. They are unpredictable events at any time, but when kids are involved they can become a kind of practical demonstration of chaos theory. A pig drive can easily turn into a contest between a young exhibitor trying desperately to keep his animal in front of the judge and a pig who is equally determined to be anywhere else. But there is more than humor in watching children show their livestock. Children participating in the work of the family lend a special dignity to that work and to the fair.

Farm people at the fair, as everywhere, are a caretaker people. Their success as breeders and exhibitors, and in many cases their well-being, depends not only on their knowledge of their animals but also on how well they care for them. At the fair the needs of the animals are always the first priority. There is no relaxation or play until those needs are met. During the fair many exhibitors move right in with their livestock, giving the barns a pleasantly disheveled look of encampment. Perhaps the fact that they must first serve the needs of other creatures for their livelihood is what gives these people their unpretentious character.

Whatever the reason, I have found the farm exhibitors and breeders to be among the most delightful people I have ever encountered—and certainly among the most fun to photograph. Most of the people I have photographed in candid situations will put on a face for the camera as though hiding or protecting something—but not these people. They look into that lens, and there is no doubt that you are seeing who they really are. There is no shame, no false pride or embarrassment, no attempt at concealment. In many cases, people, thinking that their animals are the single reason for the photograph, become so preoccupied with presenting their charges in the best light that they completely forget that they are in the photograph as well. Most of us tend to live very guarded lives in public, and the openness shown by these people is a rarity in these times. Jim Riley put it this way when describing his travels east: "I love Boston and the area, but when I get to Boston, and I start walkin' down the streets, even the women come walkin' at me with just a staunchness—that 'look out . . . I'm in control of everything here . . . don't get in my space.' And that's not the attitude that we have here."

In addition to the family exhibitors there can be found another group of people, who show their livestock at many different fairs during the year.

Commonly known as "jocks" or "roadies," they are colorful characters brimming over with stories and the fellowship of a traveling people. They have always been an important part of the fair, and though their numbers are rapidly decreasing, they can still be found in the barns and exhibition rings. If you seek them out and spend some time with them, you will not be disappointed.

Lloyd Alexander doesn't travel the exhibition circuit anymore, but he used to; for fifty years, he has shown sheep, hogs, and chickens at a multitude of fairs in dozens of states. He recalls stories of the early days when exhibitors traveled the circuit by rail.

> Back in the boxcar days in the 'teens and the twenties there were poultry people, breeders, exhibitors, even some money men, that would have a poultry farm, hire somebody to manage it, some well-known poultry person. But at fair time, they'd rent a boxcar and fix it up to haul their poultry and they'd make the show circuit. They were known as "string men," goin' from fair to fair. If they wanted some new birds from home . . . they'd call home, or write home, and tell somebody there to put certain birds on Railway Express, and if I was gonna be in Nebraska next week, "Ship 'em to Lincoln, Nebraska, a certain day, and I'll get 'em there."

String men were a favorite of the judges because they were knowledgeable and fair-minded. Problems were more likely with new exhibitors who didn't know the birds. Lloyd illustrated this by recounting a more recent occurrence in the poultry building.

> There was some new people there and the judge placed their birds last consistently and they were unhappy. They were in the office complaining. The judge was in the office trying to tell 'em how they had hatchery birds. And they weren't big enough; they weren't good enough. I can take you over there; I can pick you out hatchery birds and show 'em to you. But they didn't know the difference. So this is a part of exhibiting at fairs.

Lloyd went on to explain that judging is and always has been a rather subjective matter and that there have been times when some exhibitors were more knowledgeable than a particular judge. "We used to say when we was showin' sheep, 'Well today's over with; next week it'll be different.' But, it was that way years ago. . . . So, you know this has been goin' on ever since 1901 when the first Missouri State Fair was held. Some years you had a good judge, some years you didn't."

Jim Riley, as sheep superintendent, knows these exhibitors who travel from fair to fair well.

> JoBill Reid . . . he could tell you the older breeders. . . . They were on that circuit, and they'd start out and they would most of the time end up in Chicago at the Chicago International. They'd tell of loading all the sheep, or livestock, onto the boxcars. . . . They would complain about where they would be dropped off. . . . They'd drop those cars off, and they might be right by the carnival, or they'd have to then get all the sheep down and herd 'em to the hog barn or wherever they were being housed.

Transportation is less of a logistical burden for today's jocks who make the circuit. They travel in large pickups with double-deck stock trailers, but they are no less colorful than their predecessors. Bill Gurgin is a classic example. Always ready to laugh or share a story, he travels from state to state showing his sheep, and in the off season, he farms and does a little car racing. He was on the rodeo circuit for twelve years. He and others like him are each unique and colorful mosaics; in the words of Jim Riley,

> If you come to the fair and you don't see those people, then you've missed the fair. . . . You hear their stories about where they were broke down here or how they run out of money there . . . all the problems, but they love it. . . . It's hard to say they are not part of the crew anymore, because Bill has been comin'—all those guys, they've been comin', as long as anybody else. So the barbecues and the ice cream socials and any of the activities that we have in the nonshowing part of the day . . . those guys are invited to more of 'em than I am as superintendent. In other words, they kind of float around, and you know that ol' boy's on the road and nobody's cookin' for him.

Jim smiles as he says this, because he knows full well that the roadies are "hospitality magnets" at the Missouri State Fair.

JoBill Reid has been showing sheep for sixty-five years, and his sheep have traveled all over the country.

> I bought a trailer in '72 and the neighbors thought it was the craziest thing anybody in the country would ever do, and it

probably was. But we used it, and, funny thing, they all did, too. That trailer's hauled millions of dollars' worth of livestock for other people. But it's all the friendships . . . there's a certain amount of hard knocks goes with it, too. . . . And then there's disappointments. But, I wouldn't take anything for it. Even if I'm too old to do it now. . . . Been a lot of nights on the road. . . . My sheep have been at a lot of different places. I'm a farmer and a week or two weeks is all I've ever been able [to take off] . . . but my sheep have been from Detroit, east, [and] clear to Portland and San Francisco, Phoenix, Louisville.

One will find among the farm families and the folks who travel the circuit a code of camaraderie and fellowship. For Lloyd Alexander it goes back more than fifty years.

When I first started at the Ohio State Fair in '47 there was a great, well, I guess you'd say fellowship, comradeship, in helping somebody else. Showin' boars. At that time we showed pigs, what was known as fall boars, which were a year old; junior yearling boars, which was a year and a half old; senior yearling boars was two years old; and then aged boars, over two years old. When you get to showing those kind of animals, that's weighin' from eight-fifty to eleven hundred pounds, you need just a little bit of experience to handle them, make 'em go where you want 'em to go and keep 'em so they don't fight with another one, which they're ready to do real quick. I don't know of anybody that ever had a problem of gettin' help to show an older boar. . . .

Of course, back in my younger days, when we threshed, our neighbors came in and helped us thresh. That's wheat, oats, small grain. But when they threshed, we returned the help and went to their place. Today there's a very, very small amount of that, of course. All your grain's combined today, and you either have your own combine or you have some operator do it for you, so agriculture has changed so much. This I think has changed the background of the people that are exhibiting at the fair.

Certainly backgrounds have changed, but fortunately not the feeling of camaraderie and fellowship. And it is that very sense of camaraderie and "specialness" that binds these people together at the fair. When I mentioned the word *community*, Jim Riley responded,

In reality, that's what we form here, because every year you come back down here and you see all your friends and you sit around for four or five days and you reminisce and it's just like a family reunion in a way. People . . . they could care less what you do professionally. . . . Thomas back here is a dentist. He and his wife come and every year they'd come and he'd have about two or three old Suffolk sheep that he'd throw into the trailer . . . trim 'em down and wash 'em. . . . But he come to sit back there in the camping ground and see all of his buddies, and he was an orthodontist . . . and boy, he wasn't a dentist here by any means. You could spend ten years around him and never recognize the fact. . . . Everybody in the barn, he was friends with. And then you follow them . . . and the rest of their family, you know where they're at and what they're doing. . . . It's a community, a family, and it fits real easy.

There is even a more or less official drink among many of the exhibitors in the sheep pavilion at the Missouri State Fair. Exactly where it originated no one can say for sure, but it was introduced to the state fair by Lloyd.

When I was showin', I always showed at Columbia at the Boone County Fair, and down through the years a lot of people in that area have been sheep exhibitors. Show day they'd all bring in something for a noon picnic dinner and, of course, they'd always invite me. Well I was there one evening in the barn and Jimmy Lloyd Sapp come through . . . and he was carrying this bucket. He said, "Here Lloyd, have a drink." Well, I knew he was a number-one joker and he liked to have fun. Well, I was just a little bit gun shy of this bucket he was packin'. And I don't know, I used some kind of an excuse, and so finally he turned it up and he drunk out of it. Well, I thought, "My gosh, if he can drink out of it, I can drink out of it." Well, it turned out this was a very, very, refreshing drink. A little alcohol in it, not a lot. It didn't have enough alcohol in it that it would bother you physically or mentally. . . . You take this gallon paint bucket and fill it about half full of ice. Use three twelve-ounce cans of Mountain Dew, two cans of Sprite, a third of a fifth of VO, and then tear up a nice handful of mint leaves to put in there. Then fill the bucket up with ice and get it mixed real good. This is the recipe you use to mix this bucket. Well, they told me what to do and how to do it, and of course I was makin' a lot of fairs, so I got me a bucket and I got to mixin' buckets here and there and wherehaveya . . .

Thus began the tradition of the "Rusty Bucket" at the Missouri State Fair. According to Eloise Riley, "There was one or two guys that would partake from the bucket that chewed [tobacco]. We've never lost anybody from the bucket . . . but you didn't ever want to drink after the guy that chewed."

These fair people are a storytelling people. Evenings and quiet time are spent in each other's company telling stories of past accomplishments, the besting of a competitor in the show ring, or pranks played on others. To some the humor might occasionally seem a bit coarse, but it's rarely mean-spirited and almost always gentle. Some stories have become legends and are told again and again, year after year. As I have listened to fair people share the stories of their lives, I have come to realize that these individuals were formed and nourished in a world of intimate human contact. I fear that world is rapidly disappearing.

There is much talk these days about "values" and "ethics." The popular media constantly lament the "moral bankruptcy" of our culture, and surely there can be no doubt that many of us are trying to retain or reconnect with a sense of purpose and meaning in our lives. But what I

have found at the Missouri State Fair is that many of its people have never lost their sense of purpose or meaning. Values are so much at the core of their lives that one cannot separate value from life. Lloyd described to me the meaning of values in his life.

I am not as religious as I should be, but I have always tried to be honest in my dealings, regardless of what or who with. We've sold chickens in nineteen different states and Canada. And outside of about two or three people that we've shipped birds to, all of 'em have called and been pleased with what we sold 'em. . . . Well, it makes me feel like I'm fair to my fellow man. Good feeling inside. Of course that don't put groceries on the table, but at least I can go to bed at night and know the kind of business deal I've made don't keep me awake.

Why do we keep coming back to the fair? Nostalgia, perhaps. For me, the fair satisfies my own desire to return, for a while at least, to a place where people come together to share the rich tapestries of their lives. Almost everyone I know who grew up in the heartland has a favorite childhood or family story involving their state fair.

It has been said that there has been more change over the last twenty-five years of the twentieth century than over the first seventy-five years. Certainly much at the Missouri State Fair has changed over the past century, but just as much has not. For many people, the fair stands as an island of continuity within their own lives, between childhood and adulthood as well as different generations. The fair, which once served as a window giving early fairgoers a glimpse into the future, still sustains a vibrant present, giving us an opportunity to rediscover a people and a way of life still connected to the land.

Most of us live in a world dazzled to the point of weariness by incessant change. At the same time, we have become addicted to the predictable and uniform. It is possible to travel the length and breadth of our nation on interstate highways and see nothing regionally unique. We stay in chain motels, eat in chain restaurants, buy things in chain stores, and find entertainment in "theme parks." State fairs offer us something different. When the relentless winds of change that

blow through our lives become too much of a burden, we can still return to the fair and rediscover something we had almost forgotten, something wonderful. A place where the reality of virtue is more important than virtual reality. A place where meaning is still found in the richness of the measured moments of our lives.

I have thought a great deal over the years about the Missouri State Fair and particularly its farm people, who, as do all farmers, willingly submit to the whims of natural forces totally beyond their control. With the acceptance that they really are not in control, there seems to come a deeper level of understanding, a humility, and a gentleness uncommon in our time. I mentioned to Eloise Riley one afternoon how I marveled at this quality of acceptance, and after a moment's thought, she said simply, "It brings out the greater oneness that is there. It's a faith and an understanding, and it's putting your trust in the very best possible place. It's a real strong basis for belief."

FACES

As a photographer, I have always had an endless fascination with faces. Faces can be windows, walls, and sometimes mirrors. They are signposts, each a unique source of information. They are yesterday and tomorrow; dignity and absurdity. To read them is to learn about ourselves—the Missouri State Fair is a wonderful library of faces.

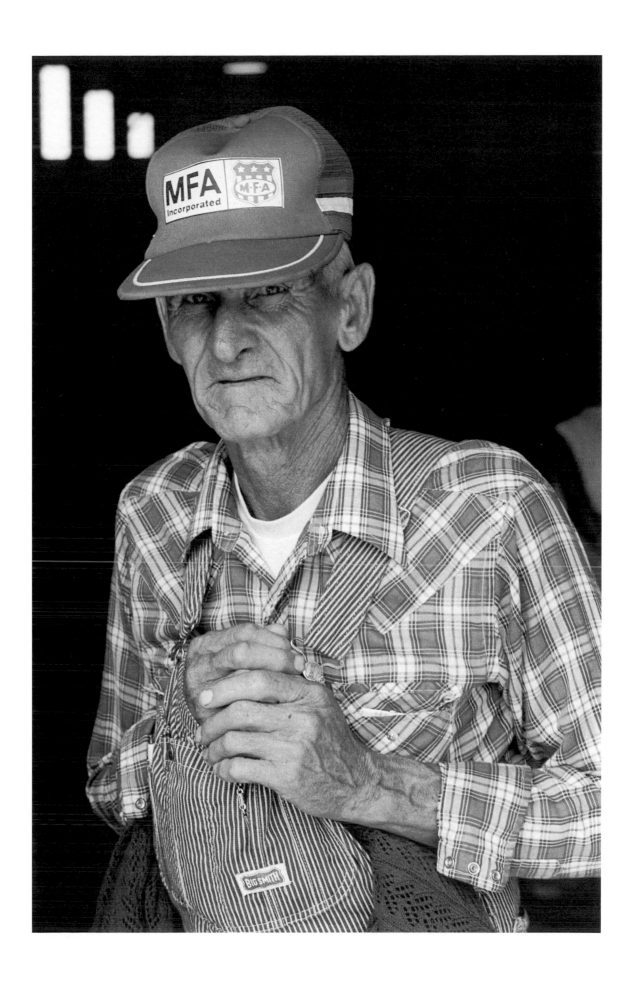

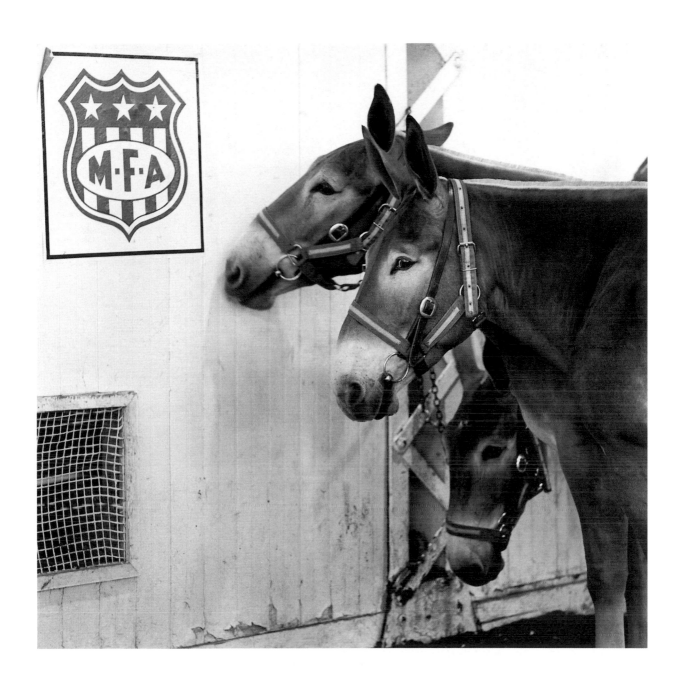

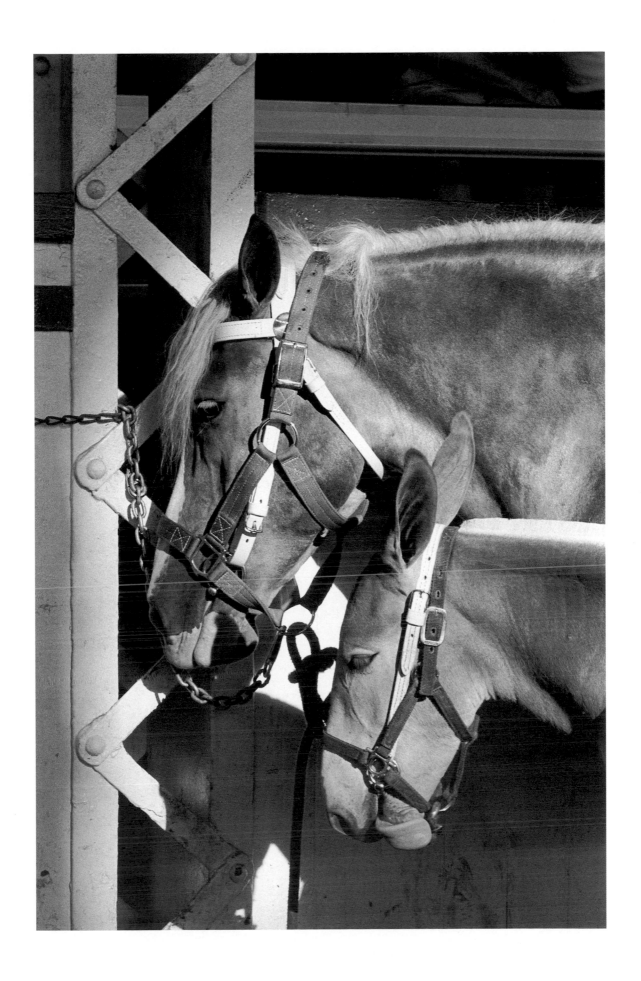

GENERATIONS

The Missouri State Fair is a place where different generations still work and play together, respect each other, and share common interests and goals. Old people still have dignity and purpose here and are frequently found in moments of quiet reflection, or sharing their experience, wisdom, and stories with younger folks. Generations are still bound together here by the land, livelihoods, and common values.

PARTNERS

For me, there is no other aspect of the fair more compelling than that partnership between humans and animals. Here you will find gentleness, respect, trust, and often genuine affection. At the fair, animals seem to bring out the best in their caretakers, and I am reminded, in this age of frozen packages in supermarkets and windowless factory farms, that living things give their lives to sustain us. That fact is still understood and respected here.

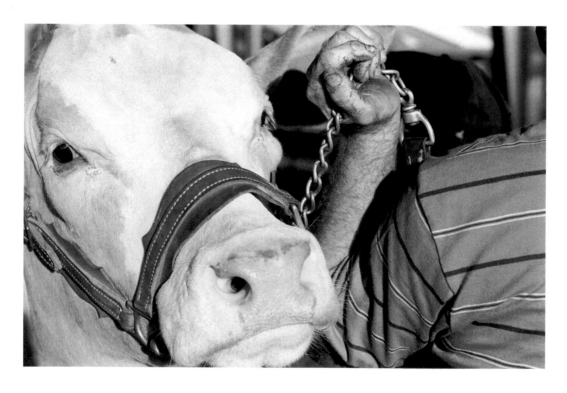

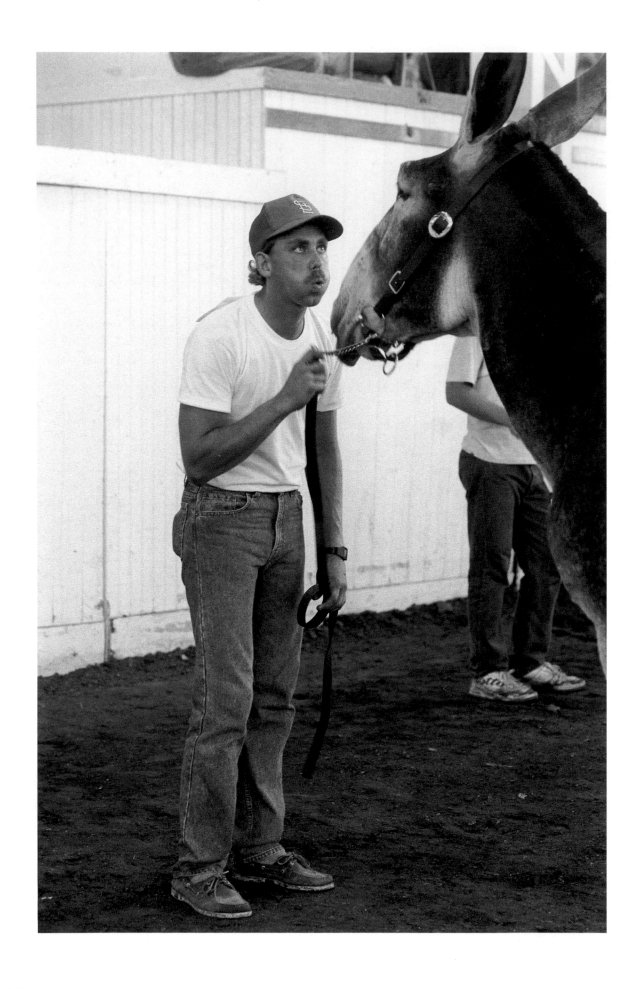

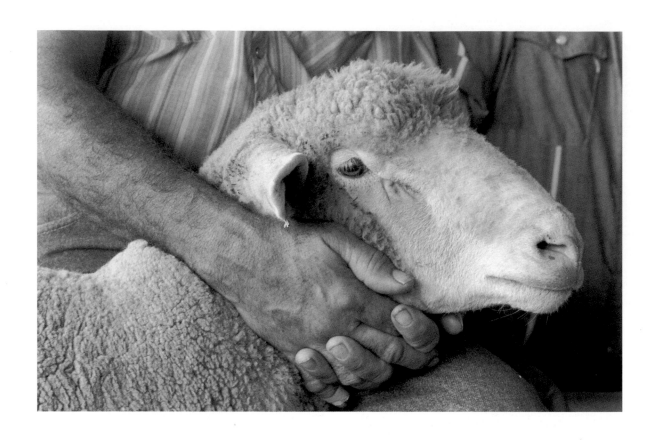

At Work, At Play

At the fair, the work of ordinary people becomes a source of delight and entertainment to many, while their play provides work for others, such as the carnies, who themselves are a source of fascination. Work and play blur together in the unique and colorful world of the state fair. In this world, memories of a lifetime are made, savored, shared, and passed from one generation to another.

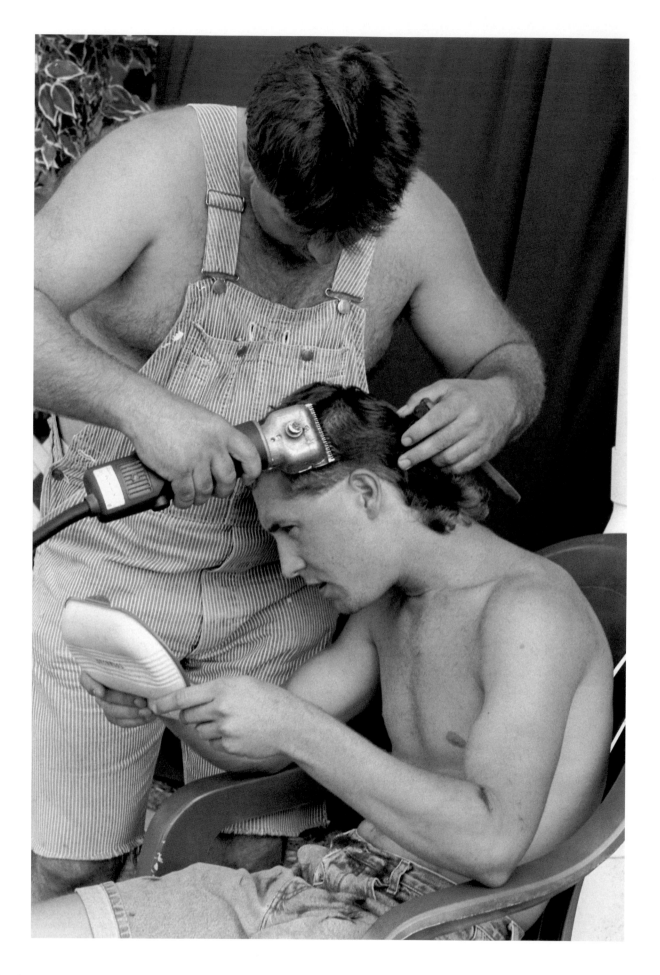

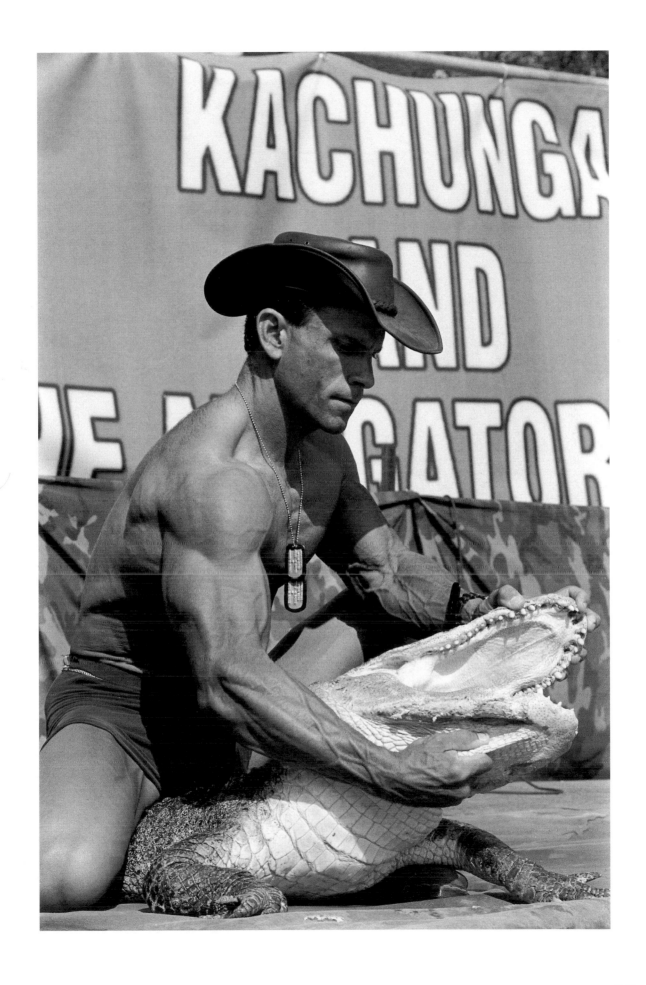

AT HOME

The buildings of the Missouri State Fair have witnessed the hopes and dreams of people for generations. Their dignity and simple elegance is a testament to the character of the people and creatures who have been their inhabitants through the years, winning, losing, striving, resting—living. If the buildings could tell us what they have seen, they would speak of extraordinary moments in the lives of ordinary people.

PHOTOGRAPHS